T0368211

I Can't Make
This Stuff Up

I Can't Make
This Stuff Up

Edward Bray

Copyright © 2024 by Edward Bray.

ISBN:	Hardcover	979-8-3694-1885-7
	Softcover	979-8-3694-1884-0
	eBook	979-8-3694-1912-0

All rights reserved. No part of this book may be reproduced or transmitted in any form or by any means, electronic or mechanical, including photocopying, recording, or by any information storage and retrieval system, without permission in writing from the copyright owner.

Any people depicted in stock imagery provided by Getty Images are models, and such images are being used for illustrative purposes only. Certain stock imagery © Getty Images.

Print information available on the last page.

Rev. date: 03/27/2024

To order additional copies of this book, contact:
Xlibris
844-714-8691
www.Xlibris.com
Orders@Xlibris.com
831374

CONTENTS

INTRODUCTION

What you are about to read are the true life experiences of a father who has miraculously survived for seventy-nine years as of this writing. You may not believe in guardian angels, but I know that they do exist. There is no other explanation for my length of days and escape from circumstances that should have caused my demise many times over.

My purpose in sharing these stories is to pass on to future generations the results of my lack of good judgment and occasional ignorance regarding the consequences of my choices.

The following recollections are dedicated to my two daughters and my wife of over fifty years. Some of these events either included them or were witnessed by them. They have been amazed at my resilience and survival of numerous near-death occurrences.

SURVIVING MY YOUTH

From the very beginning, it seemed that I was doomed to lead a perilous life. Before the age of ten, I overcame what seemed like an endless string of diseases, including (but not limited to) several bouts with different forms of measles, chicken pox, mumps, scarlet fever, and tonsillitis.

Even more amazing was my ability to survive accidents that should have killed me or maimed me for life. Allow me to demonstrate:

1. At the age of five or six, I dove off the homemade see-saw in our yard head first into the ground without breaking my neck.
2. On another occasion, I fell out of a tree and landed on my head, which resulted in an indentation in the back of my skull. This indentation took the form of a ring that became quite visible when my hair was cut short. The other kids took great delight in making fun of this "deformity" by calling me *ringworm*.
3. We used to play a game called "Stretch". You stretched out your legs and tried to throw your knife in the ground to a spot that was beyond the stretch of your opponent's legs. During one of these games, my friend accidentally threw his knife through the top of my foot.

4. When I was a teenager, I managed to fall on a rake that was on the floor of my friend's dark basement. Three of its prongs penetrated my hand.

5. As a teenager, I would mow people's lawns to earn money. While cutting someone's grass one day, a piece of metal flew out from beneath the mower and buried itself in my calf. To this day, it still resides there.

6. In fourth grade, another boy threatened to stab me with a pencil. He followed through on his threat! The lead is still embedded in the palm of my right hand.

7. While ice skating, I fell flat on my face. When I turned over, a fountain of blood shot up like a geyser! I ran home and rushed through the front door. My mother nearly fainted at the bloodied sight of me. However, like all mothers of active boys, she knew what to do. She simply squeezed the wound shut, applied a bandage across my nose, and sent me on my way. My nose remains crooked to this day.

8. When I was a young child, I rode my bike everywhere. One evening, I was riding my bicycle through a neighbor's back yard. I was going very fast, and I didn't see the clothesline across the driveway. Suddenly, it caught me just below the chin. I blacked out and was unconscious before I hit the pavement. When I came to, I found myself in my neighbor's kitchen. My mother was tending to my wounds, which were fairly extensive. My entire right side was a bloody mess! I recovered, but I never rode my bike through their back yard again.

I could go on, but I believe you now have an understanding of the necessity of my guardian angels to be on twenty-four hour watch and work in shifts.

IS SHE COMING BACK?

If you had brothers or sisters growing up, you probably experienced conflict. My sister was four years older than me and pretty much bossed me around. Needless to say, we fought a lot. When my mother would involve herself in our battles, she usually took my sister's side, which only worsened our fighting.

In regards to this particular incident, I don't remember exactly what happened- just that we were fighting as usual. My mother came into the room and was really upset with both of us. She shouted that she had enough, and she told us to go upstairs and grab our coats and gloves. We did as we were told and waited for her downstairs in the living room. When she came back downstairs, she was carrying two suitcases, which we assumed were for us. Without saying a word, she ushered us into the car. We climbed into the backseat with our suitcases. We had no clue as to what was happening.

She drove us many miles into the countryside and eventually stopped the car. She got out, opened our door, and told us to get out with our suitcases. We exited the vehicle and just stood there by the side of the road. She got back in the car and drove off. We watched it disappear out of sight. My sister and I looked at each other in utter confusion. We had been dropped off in the middle of nowhere with no houses in sight. I don't know how long we stood there, but our mother eventually returned and took us back home. We never discussed the incident again.

I'M IN THE ARMY NOW!

In 1962, I graduated from high school. Like most typical teenagers, I had no idea what I wanted to do with my life. Many of my classmates had joined the military. At the time, we were involved in a conflict in Vietnam, and many young men were likely to be drafted into either the Marines or the Army. Rather than taking a chance on being drafted, I chose to take a battery of tests given by the Army. I scored very high on all these tests, and I had my choice of which career I would pursue.

On August 6, 1962, I boarded a military bus with forty other young men in the city of Philadelphia. We were on our way to Fort Dix, New Jersey, where we would spend twelve weeks of living hell.

When we pulled up to the "welcome center", the bus door opened, and a tall, burly sergeant appeared in front of us. He started issuing commands and reminded me of a Hollywood movie sergeant. He was gruff, stern in manner and speech, and skilled in the use of profanity to the point of being irreverent. His first command was for all forty of us to exit the bus in the next thirty seconds. (We quickly learned that all commands were meant to be carried out swiftly and with unreasonable time limits.)

After getting off the bus, we marched/ran to the clothing issue center. I foolishly expected that all articles of clothing would fit perfectly. When asked what size I wore, I explained that I had no clue because my mother purchased everything I was wearing. This sergeant now became my surrogate mother. When I was issued my boots, when I told him that they were a little tight, he told me that they would loosen up after some wear. They did loosen up after several long marches, but not before I had developed large, painful blisters.

After our clothing was issued, they provided each of us with a standard issue duffel bag. One oversight that the Army made was that the bag was not large enough to hold everything we had been given. Not to worry! We were given the freedom to choose our own methods of packing. It was a comical sight to watch everyone try to accomplish this. Some kicked, shoved, or stomped with their feet. The most successful means was to have the heaviest man sit on top of the bag and squish the contents down until it could be closed.

The next step was to collect our bedding. We were each issued a wool blanket, two bed sheets, one pillow, and a pillowcase. Earlier I mentioned that we were given unreasonable time limits to complete tasks. Well, this applied directly to me at this time. The sergeant got within two inches of my face and screamed that I was not moving fast enough. My punishment was to run around the block with everything I had been given. At the time, I weighed a whopping 125 pounds. The weight of the duffel bag plus the bedding weighed nearly as much as I did! The block around which I had to run wasn't any walk in the park. It turned out to be a half mile. It was fortunate that he didn't make me do it twice because I was "too slow".

The Army was very big on "volunteering". After being in the service for about six hours, I was "volunteered" to be a food server for the evening meal. The Army had interesting names for everything related to the military. For instance, a food server was on KP, or kitchen police. Perhaps that referred to a right to bring charges of assault against a person who threw the food you served back at you. By the way, you did not get to choose your food. You ate everything you were given. All of it. It didn't take me long to go from 125 to 140 pounds during basic training.

You might be curious what we did for those twelve weeks. It's very simple. We marched and marched; then we did more marching between marches. The fun part was that the sergeant got to decide if we looked tired enough. If not, he would throw in some double time and then slow down to a forced march. A forced march was a bit slower than double time but a bit faster than marching.

The most despised and feared soldiers were usually the drill sergeants. They could be ruthless, mean-spirited, profane, irreverent, demeaning, and disrespectful. I (of course) never asked why, but they tended to enjoy putting the fear of God in you. They also may have gotten a kick out of making you wet your pants or watching you puke because they forced you to double time right after eating dinner. It could have been that some were just sadistic by nature or working towards promotions.

We had a platoon sergeant who definitely had a sadistic side. One morning at 5 a.m., we had to fall out for PT, which was physical training. Each two-story barracks held fifty men. When the sergeant blew his whistle, we had to literally run out of the barracks by the predetermined time. The soldiers on the second floor crashed into the first-floor occupants as we all tried to exit the building at the same time. Our sergeant wasn't happy with how long it took us to get into formation, so he made us go back inside. The next time, we had to carry our three-foot-wide foot lockers with us. He had to have been laughing internally, but he began to berate us for being so slow. Back inside we went, but this time we were to fall out with our mattresses. We figured that if we had had to keep going, he'd have made us carry out our bunks!

Basic training was full of all kinds of fun activities. One night, our platoon was trucked out to a remote area in Fort Dix. At sunset, we were divided into small groups of five and given topographical maps of the area. It became quite dark, and we had to use our flashlights with red lenses to look at the maps. None of us had a clue what we were looking at. (I think I had fallen asleep during the class on reading topographical maps…) Each group was given settings called *azimuths*. You were given a starting azimuth and were told how far you would go until you found a marker on the ground. From there, you were given another azimuth, and you continued on that course until you reached your final destination point.

Off we went. Each group encountered various terrain challenges. Some of the obstacles included swamps, streams, shallow lakes, or briars. Our obstacle turned out to be briars. Each man in our group would take turns going forward several yards following the designated azimuth. We would then go to the spot where he stood and repeat the process. Instead of encountering a SMALL patch of briars, we were faced with one that was about 100 yards long! I still believe that the Army planted those briars on purpose.

Fire watch was another fun activity for us recruits. Usually, we were in bed at 10:00 or 10:30 at night, and wake-up call was at 5:00 in the morning. When you were on fire watch, you were lucky to get a few hours of sleep. Come 5:00 a.m., the sergeant came in and turned on the lights. He then proceeded to wake everybody up by beating his baton on the metal bed frames and yelling obscenities at us until we got up. On one occasion, I was sleep-deprived from doing fire watch; I got up, proceeded to the latrine, and immediately took a leak in the laundry wash tub. The funny part was that no one saw me or just didn't care.

A Leisurely Drive
in Switzerland

I was stationed overseas in Germany for three years, and I was in Nuremburg for eighteen months. I was able to see many countries during that time. For one specific trip, I chose several sites in Switzerland that I wanted to see. I got into my 1949 VW and headed off.

I was having difficulty finding one of the places, so I stopped to ask for directions from a man who was walking by. Even though I couldn't speak the language, I thought I could understand enough of what he was saying to get to my destination. I thanked him and proceeded to go in the direction in which he pointed me.

Everything seemed to be going well, but the road narrowed into a much smaller paved path. I continued on, and a three-foot post suddenly appeared in the middle of the path. I quickly swerved to avoid hitting it. Rather than stop, I drove on, and patches of flowers appeared on both sides of the path. At this point, I realized that I was not on a real road- I was on someone's garden path!

Since the path was so narrow now, I had no choice but to continue moving forward. What had been a flat path began to descend steeply. A normal person would probably have stopped and backed up. I was and am not a normal person. I was once told that common sense and intelligent go hand-in-hand, but I have shattered that myth.

Just when I thought the worst was over, it got worse. What appeared before my eyes was a flight of stairs that continued my descent about a hundred feet to the street below. There was no turning back, so down I went. The car was difficult to steer as it bounced all over the place, but I managed to make it to the street. I can't imagine what expressions people had on their faces as my car appeared out of nowhere in front of them. I was very fortunate to have only lost my muffler on this adventure!

Near Death in
the Alps

Have you ever been involved in a situation where it nearly resulted in your own death? In 1965, I was taking a week off for my leave and decided to attend an international Bible camp in the beautiful Alps of southern Germany.

No events were scheduled over the weekend, so two friends and I decided to climb one of the tall mountains that was close to us. We had no ropes or climbing gear because we had planned a leisurely outing.

We drove to the base of the mountain in my 1949 Volkswagen. The weather was fairly mild with partly cloudy skies. The temperature was about 40 degrees Fahrenheit, but we didn't think too much about our attire; we were expecting to be gone for a couple of hours. According to our map, the mountain was a little over 11,000 feet in elevation, and it didn't seem to us that it would be a difficult or steep hike.

Wearing street clothes and regular shoes, the three of us started hiking. We didn't plan on going to the peak because of our limited time, but we did hope to get a good view of Hitler's Eagle's Nest.

Our ascent hadn't seemed very steep; however, when we turned around, it was obvious that it was way too steep to go back the way we had come. One of my friends had been a mountain guide in the United States. As a matter of fact, I had trained with him when we had been stationed near the Rocky Mountains. He told us that he could find an easier way to descend, so we started heading in an easterly direction until we could start heading down. We made good progress until we came to a very steep cliff. This is where the story becomes truly terrifying.

Our friend and guide lowered himself over the edge of the cliff and slowly made his way down. I followed and made sure that I was placing my feet exactly where he had placed his. To say that I was scared stiff would be an understatement. As I was clinging to the side of the mountain with my body pressed against the rock face, I was trembling uncontrollably to the point I thought I was going to fall. I was literally supporting myself with my fingertips and the tips of my shoes. Our situation worsened.

We came to what I referred to as a "chimney", or a vertical gap between rock faces. We had to brace our backs against one face and extend our feet horizontally to make contact with the opposite side of the gap. Fortunately, the gap was shallow, and we were able to negotiate the section successfully. The worst was soon to come.

After exiting the gap, we came to a place with better footing. Our guide was below me on the mountain; I was just a few feet above him. Our other friend was several feet above me. As I was looking down to see where I should place my feet next, I heard blood-curdling scream coming from above. Our friend had lost his grip, fell past me, and almost knocked our guide off the mountain. He continued falling and had turned completely upside down. We heard his head hit rock; it sounded like someone had dropped a watermelon onto the pavement. His body left a trail of blood as it slid across a snow field. A boulder kept him from plunging into a dark abyss that turned out to be a drop of over a thousand feet. We couldn't believe it when he stood up! We yelled down to him, and he let us know that he was all right. It took us about forty-five minutes to reach him.

When we did, we were met with a gruesome sight: the side of his head was sliced open. It looked like someone had taken a meat cleaver and sheared off a slice of his skull. Several of his front teeth had been knocked out, and his shoes had disappeared somewhere in the snow field. I had lost one of my shoes, as well; we never did find any of them.

As we were helping our friend, it began to rain. We were soon soaking wet and shivering in our woefully inadequate jackets. It was determined that our guide would go down the rest of the way and try to find help. Meanwhile, I tried to keep our fallen friend warm by hugging him close to my body. We laid there in the snow for several hours before we heard the rescue team coming. It was about two o'clock in the morning. Our guide had been fortunate to come across Swiss and German rescue teams that had been looking for us. Our camp supervisor had reported us missing. If it hadn't been for our guide, they never would have found us; they were almost a mile from where we actually were on the mountain.

The first thing that they did was get us dried off by removing our clothing and wiping us down with towels. We were then wrapped in blankets, strapped onto rescue sleds, and gradually pulled and lowered to the bottom of the mountain where ambulances waited to rush us to the hospital. Suffering from double exposure, I remained there for a couple of days. My friend stayed there for several more days while they saw to his needs. I never did see or hear from him again. I still have the newspaper article that they wrote about us. I never knew what it said because it was written in German. My oldest daughter helped translate it for me over fifty years later.

FROM BAVARIA

wedding   K Mh Guttenberg

The eldest daughter of the CSU Bundestag member Freiherr von und zu Guttenberg, the 20-year-old Elisabeth Reichsfreiin von und zua Guttenberg, was married in Stadtsteinach to Franz Ludwig Schenk Graf von Stauffenberg, 27-year-old son of Claus Schenk Graf von Staufenberg, who was executed after the assassination attempt on Hitler. fenberg, married in a civil ceremony. The church wedding takes place today in the Schloßkirche zua Guttenberg near Stadtsteinach. The young couple will live in Oberpframmern near Munich.

Crashed while taking photos

Two poorly equipped Americans fell about 20 meters deep while photographing chamois in the Hoher Göll area near Berchtesgaden. The injured lay helpless at the scene of the accident for hours because the mountain rescue service was not contacted until late by a third American. They had to be taken to the hospital with severe hypothermia.

Over 4000 carrier pigeons missing

The racing pigeon breeders of Wiesbaden and Mainz are faced with a puzzle: 4,700 racing pigeons that were picked up in Passau on Saturday morning to fly back to their home lofts.

I'M IN THE
JAILHOUSE NOW!

While I was stationed overseas, I worshipped with a small congregation in the city of Nuremberg. I made several friends and kept in contact with them for many years after returning to the U.S.

In 1964, I was moving from Abilene, Texas, to Los Angeles, California. On my way through Texas, I decided to stop and visit one of my friends from Nuremberg. I pulled into their driveway and walked up to their front door. I knocked several times, but there was no answer. A patrol car quietly pulled up to the house, and a police officer got out of the car. He approached while I was still peering through the front window and startled me. He inquired as to why I was looking in someone's window, and I explained that I was just visiting a friend from overseas. He then informed me that the house into which I was looking had been broken into just a few days prior. The officer told me that I had to follow him into town to verify my story with the friend.

It is important to understand that I was having some problems with my transmission; I had somehow lost one of the gears- reverse. Once we arrived at the jail, the officer wanted me to back into a specific parking spot. Since my car was incapable of this maneuver,

I made a U-turn in the middle of the road. After I had parked, the officer asked me why I had done that in front of him. Without the intention of humor or sarcasm, I replied that I didn't have a functional reverse gear in my car. His immediate response was to commandeer my car keys and wallet, and I was required to sleep in my car overnight next to the station. After a sleepless night in my car, the sheriff returned my keys and wallet and bid me farewell before I continued on to California.

COUNSELOR AND MENTOR

I've probably given you the impression that I'm not a responsible individual. It isn't that I'm not responsible; it's just that I sometimes (or maybe quite often) am oblivious to the potential consequences of my actions. You could also surmise that I don't always act like an adult. There is a reason for this. I was brought up by a very strict mother, so my choices were often the result of rebellion against her suppression of my will. After leaving the nest, my real self was allowed to blossom, which occasionally resulted in some embarrassing and somewhat humorous events.

I was going to college in 1966, and I dated a girl who talked me into serving as a counselor at a Christian summer camp for junior high boys and girls. In my cabin were ten young boys in my charge. At some point during one day, several girls had snuck into our cabin while we were away. They had weaved toilet paper through the beams and bunk beds before hosing it all down using the fire extinguisher in the cabin.

I chose not to take this action lying down. I mustered my young charges, and we devised a plan of retaliation against those responsible for the attack. Our plan was to take pails of water and soak the offending girls while they slept. Like the charge of the light brigade, we raced across the compound at full speed with me leading the pack. Little did we know that the camp superintendent was witnessing our movements from his front door. Surprisingly, he made no effort to stop our act of revenge. It turned out the girls had locked their screen door, so we were unable to complete our mission. The next morning, I was summoned to his office and reminded that I was to be a role model for the young men instead of a rebel with misguided actions. It's a good thing that he was unaware of the skinny dipping incident that had occurred earlier...

A Heroic Act

I believe that most people live uninteresting lives. In all likelihood, an individual may never do anything that distinguishes himself/herself. Every once in a while, however, circumstances will offer a once-in-a-lifetime opportunity. That is what happened to me when I was a sophomore in college.

At Michigan Christian Junior College, I was a member of the choir. We performed at our chapel services and various venues around the States. On this particular occasion, we were traveling to Nashville, Tennessee, to make a recording at the Parthenon.

We stopped in Indiana to perform a concert at a church. Afterwards, we were loading our equipment onto the buses. I was standing at one of the large windows while I watched the loading process. Suddenly, I saw something that horrified me- a car was backing up, and a small boy was in its path! The driver couldn't see him because he was so small. Without hesitation, I ran out the door screaming at the top of my lungs for the driver to stop. Fortunately, he did. I told him to turn off the car so that it wouldn't accidentally move. By then may people had seen what was happening. The little boy was wedged under the rear of the car, and his head was just behind the rear wheel. I told the man to get out and unlock the trunk in order to retrieve the car jack, but before he could do that, a number of onlookers took it upon themselves to simply lift the rear of the car high enough so that I could pull the little boy to safety. After my heroic act, I re-entered the church building, went to the men's room, and was sick to my stomach.

I never mentioned this act to any of my friends or family. I was satisfied just to know that I had saved another human being's life.

THE CONSEQUENCES
OF A DEVOTED CAT

In 1968, I was attending Worcester Junior College and living in nearby Marlborough, Massachusetts. My wife and I lived in a one-hundred-year-old house; we had a small, four-room apartment on the third floor. I spent considerable hours in the study doing my homework every night. As such, I ate most of my dinners in that room.

At this point of the story, allow me to introduce our cat, Spanky. He was my constant companion and always wanted to be where I was in the apartment, but he managed to get into predicaments with ease. For example, my wife and I were watching television one evening while Spanky sat on the sill of a screened window. At one point, I casually looked over and was alarmed to see that the cat AND the screen were both gone! I sprinted over to the window and looked down. With surprise and relief, I saw that Spanky was still clinging to the screen that was lying on the ground. I don't know how he managed to stay on top of the screen, but it was proof to me that cats really do land on their feet.

One night, I was in the study doing my physics homework. My wife brought my dinner to me, setting the plate of spaghetti on my desk before leaving the room. I was looking forward to it because it was one of my favorite meals, and my wife always used a lot of sauce.

Suddenly and without warning, Spanky came charging into the room, leapt up on the desk, and landed exactly in the middle of my plate of spaghetti. Immediately and without forethought, I tried to grab him. Evading my grasp, he raced around the room with me in pursuit. Because his paws were coated in spaghetti sauce, he left prints all over the floor, the cabinets, the bookshelves, and my physics homework.

The next day, I handed in my homework with Spanky's paw prints all over the pages. The professor looked inquisitively at me; I simply said, "Don't ask!"

Summer Shower

When I was about twenty-three years old, I was attending Harding College in Arkansas. At the time, my wife and I didn't have any children. I didn't have a scholarship, so I worked part-time to help pay for my education. It was hard to find a job because the nearby town was so small. I was eventually hired at a car wash for a whopping seventy-five cents per hour. I worked for two hours a day, seven days a week.

One summer day, a police cruiser came in, and I turned on the machinery to start the pre-wash cycle. I suddenly realized that I had forgotten about the six-foot-tall antenna on the back end of the car. I raced to the rear of the vehicle just in time to keep it from becoming entangled in the arm of the washing mechanism. I stood there and held the antenna down so that the arm could pass over it. I remained in place as the pre-wash, soap, and rinse cycles were completed.

As I stood there, the two policemen in the car were laughing hysterically at the sight of me. Fortunately, it was extremely hot, so the cold water felt pretty good.

ALLOW ME TO DEMONSTRATE

When I graduated from Harding, I obtained a teaching certificate along with my degree in biology. My wife and I relocated to Edinboro, Pennsylvania, with our firstborn daughter. It was a small, rural farming community of 5000 people, and it only had three traffic lights. After working a variety of jobs, I interviewed for a position as an eighth grade earth science teacher in a town close to Edinboro.

At some point, we were studying volcanoes and how they erupted. One of the suggested projects was to construct a working model of an active volcano. To simulate the eruption, one of the options was to use baking soda. I thought the reaction produced would not be exciting enough for my students to witness. I don't remember how, but I managed to obtain potassium nitrate, charcoal, and sulfur. I later found out that these ingredients combined to produce an explosive reaction. And gunpowder.

I constructed my volcano at home. I used cement to form the mountain. For the core, I used an iron pipe. On Monday, I took the completed volcano to my first period class. Not knowing what would happen when the volcano exploded, I made a fortuitous decision: I had all the students in the front row move to the back of the classroom.

I took the different chemicals and poured them one by one into the iron pipe. The last thing I did was put on my safety glasses before pouring sulfuric acid into the cone. (The sulfuric acid's purpose was to create a reaction with the chemicals.)

As I poured the acid, the volcano emitted a crackling sound, soon followed by flames shooting from the cone. I immediately pulled back from the volcano just before a tremendous flame shot forth. The eruption was so violent that it shot all the way up to the ceiling! Fortunately, the ceiling panels did not catch fire.

The classroom was spared; however, I was not. I began to feel a burning sensation on the front of my chest. As I looked down, I was amazed to see holes appearing in my shirt and tie. Apparently, sulfuric acid had splattered on my clothes. Without hesitation, I tore off my tie, shirt, and even my undershirt. The boys' bathroom happened to be nearby, so I sprinted across the hallway with my entire class in tow. I doused myself with water to stop the burning of the acid. Within minutes, the school principal joined us in the crowded space. After seeing my condition, he sent me home.

When I came back the next day, I entered the classroom to see my clothing remnants pinned to the bulletin board. I imagine the students who witnessed the event still talk about it to this day.

CUTTING THE CORDS

After the birth of our second daughter in 1973, I casually asked my wife if we should try for a son. Without hesitation, her reply was that we already had a son. She was referring to me, which left me with little doubt that there would be no more additions to our family of four. Reluctantly, I agreed to have a vasectomy. It was fortunate that I didn't read about the procedure ahead of time, or I might have changed my mind. Like a lamb to the slaughter, I made my appointment, completely ignorant regarding what was going to take place.

As the doctor prepared for the operation, he said that he was going to give me a shot that would make me "not feel a thing". That was a fabrication of epic proportions. It was one of the largest needles I had ever seen! It not only hurt, but it did nothing for the pain that I would have to endure during the vasectomy.

I will avoid sharing the gruesome details, but I will say that I never thought the procedure would end. I discovered that the assistant was there to protect the doctor from my wrath, as well as to provide support for me as I gripped her arm in pain. I'm surprised that she didn't pass out from the pressure that I applied to her forearm. Later on, I asked my wife if she heard my screaming from the waiting room. She heard nothing. I'd be willing to bet that they put up extra soundproofing to keep patients' cries from reaching the ears of the next potential victims. I honestly felt like the doctor was yanking out my innards! There was a snip, and the procedure was done. Or so I thought. A feeling of relief washed over with me until the doctor said, "Okay, now for the other side!"

My Descent Into Madness

When I was in high school, I was very interested in athletic events. I participated in cross-country running and track and field. As a matter of fact, I also competed in football, wrestling, and gymnastics. I achieved some success in each of these sports, but my greatest love was cross country.

In the early 1980s, I began running ultras. An ultra race is any running event that is 31 miles or longer. I had competed in several marathons, but they didn't seem to be challenging enough. After some time, I ran my very first ultra, which was 31 miles. After completing that race, I felt the need to run even longer races. Thus, the anecdote that you are about to read describes my first attempt at running a race that was 72 miles in length.

The race was held in the Appalachian Mountains in southwestern Pennsylvania. Why I would even consider such an undertaking is beyond reason. Never the less, I plunged headlong into this attempt. I never considered what obstacles might present themselves during the race:

1. Rocks. Buried halfway in the ground, they prepared to scrape flesh from ankle bones.

2. Sticks. Placed strategically on the trail by forest elves for the sole purpose of piercing shoes and/or shins, or (better yet) entangling pairs of feet, causing spectacular head-long spills onto rocks lying in wait.

3. Rain! Not just drizzles, but repetitive, torrential downpours that conjured up flashbacks of Noah's flood. Rains that worked in collusion with roots to cause increasingly spectacular falls.

4. Lightning! Imagine being at the very top of a mountain in a lightning storm. You're running underneath a 20,000 volt power line across an open field. It was the only time that I actually sprinted during the whole race.

5. Pain! Pain in my feet from abrasions, bruises, blisters, and contusions. (After some long ultras, I had to go to my doctor to have my toes pierced to release the pressure that had built up under the toenails.) There was also the indescribable pain in my "quads", brought on by braking on kamikaze plunges into deep mountain ravines and lactic acid build-up from muscle fatigue.

In addition to the hazards created by Mother Nature and her band of forest elves, there were even more delights along the race course. For example, I carried an "indestructible" flashlight with me that lasted exactly 30 seconds. I dropped it on a rock lying in wait and immediately found myself in darkness. How dark was it? Imagine being in the basement of your house with no visible light. It seemed the bulb did not carry the same guarantee of indestructability as the flashlight itself. Try changing a lightbulb in the dark.

When you run an ultra, you almost assuredly experience fatigue, which has the capacity to produce some lovely side effects. When you run 72 miles, you don't have time to sit down to a scrumptious meal. You "pig out" on ham and cheese sandwiches, cake, and power bars (or cardboard covered in chocolate and nuts). All of these edibles are then washed down by gallons of a special runners' drink- a refreshing and replenishing lime-flavored turpentine. This trail ambrosia and beverage combo provides several hundred calories, but your body is burning 500 to 700 calories per hour. Incidentally, this is a great way to lose from 5 to 10 pounds of weight in one day.

You might ask, "What effect does this have on you?" Well, I'll tell you. You become very tired. In fact, you become so tired that you have hallucinations. On one stretch of the trail late in the race, I saw a pumpkin growing in the middle of the trail. (It turned out to be a cleverly disguised large rock waiting to ambush.) Later, I saw a go-cart, which seemed particularly odd since there was no civilization within a reasonable distance of where the race took place. As it turned out, it was two elephantine tree trunks laid precisely together across the trail by forest elves.

Those phantasmic illusions paled in comparison to those observed by another runner, who related to me that he saw two chickens walking side by side in the middle of the trail. (Perhaps they were on their way to Noah's Ark!) Not surprisingly, he dropped out at the next checkpoint.

Continuing my romp through the woods and fields, I came across another runner who seemed to be wandering around. I stopped to see if she needed any assistance. As I spoke with her, it became apparent that she disoriented. I also noticed that her body was shivering; she was suffering from hypothermia. As I spoke with her, she asked me where she was and if I was also in the race. I thought that was strange because not only was I dressed in running gear, but my race number was attached to my shirt. I finally convinced her to follow me to the next checkpoint, and she dropped out of the race.

During my years of running ultras, I was admitted to hospitals at least twice with hyperthermia from temperatures in the 80s and 90s. In one race, I lost 11 pounds in the first 25 miles. Why would a person put his/her body through such an ordeal? I believe my wife hit the nail on the head when she stated that all ultra-runners suffered from some kind of brain damage.

AIRBORNE

The town in which my family and I lived was both a summer and winter resort town 20 miles inland from Lake Erie. At the northern end of Edinboro was a large lake on which people boated and fished. In the winter, the lake was great for ice fishing. The town also had a ski hill with a tow rope. Along with ski runs, there was a five-lane tube slope.

Anyone living near the Great Lakes is familiar with the term "lake effect snow". Winters are long and severely cold. The average snowfall in our area was somewhere between 165 inches and 250 inches per winter. The first snows of the season could begin in early October and last into late April. Our last day for a frost was typically Memorial Day. The average high during February was 28°F, and the growing season for crops was 90 days. Storms usually lasted two or three days. Sunshine was a rare commodity during the months of October through March. Schools seldom closed for snow days, and I recall our daughters having to go to school when there were ONLY 12 inches of snow on the ground. One day, I had to drive to work with 18 inches of snow on the road.

Whenever there was an actual school closing, my youngest daughter, Theresa, and I would head for the town's only hill designated for sledding. It wasn't particularly steep, but it did have a nice slope of about 300 feet. I had one of those primo sleds with three skis and a steering wheel. On one occasion, Theresa and I decided to go sledding. After a while, several kids constructed a ramp to add some excitement to our experience. My daughter and I mounted our sled with her seated in the rear. Without telling her what I was about to do, I purposely steered our sled towards the ramp. The sled went up the ramp, and we were launched into the air! Since my daughter was unprepared for that maneuver, she immediately fell off the sled and continued rolling down the hill. Because the sled was now lighter, I continued (airborne) down the hill, all the while gaining speed. When the sled finally hit the ground, the impact caused the front ski to shatter, leaving just the strut. The strut got stuck in the snow, which sent my body flying over the front of the sled. I landed on my face and continued this way to the bottom of the hill. My daughter caught up to me and inquired with some concern if I was all right.

"Yes! I'm fine," I answered, surprised that I actually was.

Having witnessed that spectacular crash, she told me that what happened reminded her of a comic strip from "Calvin and Hobbes".

WHO NEEDS A SLED?

As I mentioned previously, the winters in Edinboro were long, cold, and very snowy. We often experienced blizzards that produced two or more feet of snow at one time. We lived in a split-level home, and from time to time I would have to climb up a ladder to clear the snow off the roof. On one particular occasion, three feet of snow had accumulated at the peak. That much snow was capable of crushing the eaves supporting the roof. I first removed the snow from the lower part of the roof before proceeding up to the peak. It was very cold that day. As I removed the snow down to the shingles, the moisture on them immediately froze. Without warning, I lost my balance, fell on my back, and began sliding down the pitched roof. There was no way I could stop myself, so I mentally prepared for the finale. Fortunately, the front yard was clear of objects that could harm me, so I landed in three feet of snow without any harm done to my body.

You would think that I would have learned a lesson from this near-death experience. Not so! The snow had to be removed from the other side of the roof. Up the ladder I went with shovel in glove. Once again, I removed the snow from the lower part and proceeded up to the peak. Surprise! After the snow was cleared away, the roof became just as slippery as the other side had been. What are the odds of that happening? I slipped, fell on my back, and slid towards the back yard. Our back yard was very different from the front yard. Close to the back of the house were the following: a large water tank, a triple clothes line, a small, fenced vegetable garden complete with stakes (even in winter), and a strawberry patch with metal edging. Landing on any one of those could have resulted in entanglement, major injury, or impalement. I somehow managed to land in the snow in the one, small clear area of the yard.

There had been a little bit of foreshadowing regarding the event. Two weeks prior, I had also been shoveling snow off the roof. My older daughter, Jennifer, came outside with her camera. When I asked her what she was doing, she replied that she was just waiting to take an action shot of me as I slid off the roof.

Incidentally, that was the last time I attempted to clear snow by climbing up on the roof. I purchased one of those long-handled roof shovels and remained safely on the ground.

THE BODY IN THE POND

I was a member of the Edinboro Volunteer Fire Department for ten years. I saw many horrible accidents; some of which resulted in the loss of lives.

During my tenure, I received several weeks of intensive training in Scuba Rescue Diving. On my very first rescue attempt, we received a call that a car was found sunk in a small pond. When we arrived, we saw that the car (a jeep), was completely submerged in about ten feet of water. The car had been discovered by a man who had gone there to go fishing.

I donned my wet suit, strapped on my air tanks, and dove into the almost clear water. When I got to the car, I was frightened by what I observed. A young man was sitting in the driver's seat; he was still buckled in. His eyes were open, and his skin was the color of ashes. (The coroner later determined that he had been in the pond for several days.) His whole body was bloated, giving it a very grotesque appearance.

We had to get the jeep out of the pond before we could extract the victim from his position in the front seat. I attached a tow cable to the bumper, and the vehicle was slowly pulled from its watery grave. After examining the body, the coroner wrote up his report; he surmised that the young man had most likely been drinking to excess, passed out, and fallen forward in his seat.

After the shifter was pushed into drive, the jeep rolled down the sloped embankment and was submerged, causing the young man to drown.

I had many nightmares about this experience.

FLAT EDDIE

For a while, I served as a Fire Police Lieutenant in Edinboro's all-volunteer fire department. The fire police section was composed of several volunteers plus three officers: a captain and two lieutenants. Our duties involved directing and detouring traffic around accident scenes, assisting in helicopter landings and EMT calls, and pedestrian control.

The ski resort on the outskirts of town had one downhill slope, plus a section that was dedicated strictly to tubing. The slope itself was steep and featured a vertical drop of three hundred feet.

Once a year, everyone in the fire department was invited to the ski slope for a day of skiing and tubing. The tubing hill consisted of several lanes that were separated by mounds of snow to keep each tube in its own lane.

There were two sizes of tubes to choose from: a small one for just one person or a huge one that held up to four people. Five of us decided to have a race down the slope. At the top of the hill, I set myself in my small tube while the other four piled into a larger one. We pushed off at the same time and headed downhill, gradually picking up speed. I don't know how it happened, but somehow my tube leapt over the barrier of snow between my lane from the adjacent lane.

As I flew over the barrier, I was flung from my tube and ended up on the ground. When I looked up, I was horrified to see my friends' tube hurtling towards me. There was no way they would be able to avoid flattening me. Like a colossal wave breaking on the shore, their huge tube rolled over me as if I was not even there. To this day, I cannot believe that I wasn't seriously injured. Once again, I had escaped death.

Ride It In, Pack It Out

I loved to ride my bike. In the 1950s, our home in Horsham, Pennsylvania, was surrounded by what were mostly farming communities. As a young man, I would take long bike rides through the countryside.

It was only natural that I took up competitive biking when I was in my thirties. The races I entered tended to be in mountainous terrain and were between six and fifty miles. Many of the races had hills that were so steep that it was necessary to carry your bike uphill at times. The mountain trails also had lots of rocks and tree roots. My favorite races were held in Punxatawney, Pennsylvania, the home of the famous Punxatawney Phil. The course was very hilly and had steep slopes into and out of ravines.

In one particular fifty kilometer race, I was descending down one of these kamikaze slopes when a sharp curve suddenly appeared. I knew immediately that I was in trouble, so I took actions to lessen the impact of the impending disaster. I made the huge mistake of hitting both the front and rear brakes simultaneously, activating the laws of physics.

The front brake caused the bike to come to an immediate stop while the rear tire continued its momentum upward. When the bike was fully vertical, I was able to escape serious injury by letting go of the handle bars and allowing myself to be tossed from the seat. I rolled for several feet before coming to a stop.

Somewhat bloodied and bruised, I walked back to my damaged bike that was lying in a heap. I observed that both wheels were twisted out of shape. I still had eight miles to go, so I tried jumping on each tire to straighten them out as much as I could.

Even though I only had one gear and had to carry my bike up every hill, I actually managed to complete the race.

Do You Smell Smoke?

As a fire policeman, we are on call whenever we are not at work. This includes the evening hours. We also attend meetings and drills one evening each week. One such evening, we received a 9-1-1 call that a house was on fire. Somehow, I had missed hearing the number of the house, but I had heard the name of street- my street!

As a rule, we do not go to the actual house, but we position our rescue vehicle at the end of the road to block any nonemergency traffic from obstructing the flow of fire trucks and ambulances to the scene. So when I arrived at the scene of the fire, I positioned my vehicle at the end of the street, which just so happened to be the street on which I lived. I was completely oblivious to the fact that it was my own house that was on fire! I was not told that it was my own house until I had been there for about 30 minutes. When I found out, I immediately rushed down to the scene. The fire had already been extinguished, and my wife was standing outside in her night robe; she was visibly shaken. My neighbor was also standing there, and he related to me what had taken place.

He said that he was out walking his dog when he saw flames engulfing the siding of our front porch. He immediately called 9-1-1, and the fire trucks arrived very quickly to the scene. Before they arrived, the flames had spread to a good portion of the porch.

You may wonder where my wife was during this. Believe it or not, she was taking a shower and was completely unaware that the house was on fire! I asked her what she thought was happening with all of the commotion outside. She replied, "I thought it was the television."

In any case, we discovered what had started the fire in the first place. My wife had cleaned the ashes out of the fireplace, put them in a metal pail, and placed it on the front porch. Apparently, the ashes were still smoldering and eventually caught fire. The siding began to burn, and the fire spread from there.

Thankfully, no one was injured, and the fire damage was kept to a minimum- about $800. Lesson learned: no more placing hot ashes in a metal pail!

That Was an Understatement

Our house in Edinboro was outside of town. There were no sidewalks and no curbs. But there were ditches on opposite sides of the small, two-lane road leading home. And a fairly sizable hill enroute.

In order to get to that two-lane road, we had to drive up the short hill at the top of our street. Following a snowstorm or when the hill was iced over, it became very difficult to successfully get our car onto that road. If there was traffic, we had to come to a complete stop, which meant backing down our little hill until we reached a point at which it was possible to move forward again. On several occasions, we had to do this three or four times before even having the opportunity to attempt steering onto the two-lane road. If not performed with precision, we would wind up sliding into the ditch on the other side of the road.

One winter day, my wife came home without the car, and I asked her what happened.

"I'm afraid that the car is stuck in a snowdrift and is slightly off the road."

"No problem!" I said.

Shovel in hand, I headed down the road to dig the car out of the drift. I approached the place where I expected to see it, but it was nowhere in sight. At the time, I thought some kind soul had dug the car out and pushed it out of harm's way. I was wrong. It was further down the road at the bottom of the big hill. My shovel was not going to be much help. The car was in the ditch and turned completely on its passenger side. I found out later that a passing driver had helped my wife climb up and out of the car.

THERE'S SOMETHING
ABOUT DOORS AND
ELEVATORS

I have a love-hate relationship with elevators, sliding doors, and revolving doors. Mostly hate. I truly believe the feeling is mutual.

The first incident occurred when I was working at the post office in Edinboro. The main entrance led to a vestibule where individual post office boxes were located. Just inside the main entrance to the left was a second set of double doors for people wanting to mail packages or purchase stamps from a clerk. The third door in the vestibule area was restricted access for postal employees. On this particular occasion, I was working alone on a Sunday afternoon. As I exited the employee-only door, it closed behind me. I had forgotten to unlock it, and I didn't have a key for that door or the customer door. I decided to go around to the back of the post office to open the door with the key that I did have. Then I remembered that I couldn't even exit the main door because it was also locked. I was trapped in the vestibule. There were many windows, but they only opened a little bit. I tried to get the attention of passersby for quite a while before someone saw me

---

44

through the window motioning for help. I was able to direct him to a colleague's nearby house and was soon freed.

Another time, I had an issue with a revolving door at an airport. My wife and I were returning home from a diving vacation in the Caribbean. We landed in Puerto Rico and were changing airlines for our final flight home. We each had a couple of bags plus one large bag containing our dive gear. To get to our connection, we had to go through a revolving door. I entered first with three bags. As soon as I was completely enclosed, the door stopped revolving. I was trapped. At first my wife laughed, but then she started to panic. Not because I was trapped, mind you. She was concerned that we would miss our flight. It was several minutes before airport security responded to my plight. They tried several times to force the door open but were unsuccessful. Finally, a hulk of an airport employee came to assist. He pushed and shoved and finally gave up. He determined that the only way to free me was to get a key to unlock the door. Problem- there was only one person with a key to the revolving door, and he was elsewhere on the island. Things were becoming critical at this point with only twenty-five minutes until our flight. The hulk came back and let us know that no one was coming to release me from my fishbowl. I was quite the spectacle. With all of his might, he tried once more and was able to force the door open just enough to get me (and my bags) out in time to make our connection home.

A third incident took place at a hospital as I was attempting to leave. I went through the first sliding door without any issues, and the second one was supposed to open automatically, as well. Nope! On the door was a metal bar that said, "In an emergency, hit this bar." I did. Nothing happened. I hit the bar two more times. Still nothing. I turned around to re-enter the hospital, but now that door wouldn't open. I was trapped. I banged on the door to get someone's attention. When a nurse came over to me, I told her the doors wouldn't open. I was told that the electricity had gone out, so I might be stuck for a while. I couldn't have been more unlucky.

What were the odds of the electricity going out exactly as I was between two sets of doors? Fortunately, I only had to wait about thirty minutes before the power came back on.

A fourth and final occurrence took place in a malfunctioning elevator. Guess where. Yes, in a hospital. I was on the lowest level and had to go up to the third floor. I pressed the button and the door closed; however, the elevator did not begin its ascent. I pressed the button again, but there was still no movement. Not a problem. Elevators have safety features for sticky situations. I pushed the button labeled for emergency use. Nothing happened. I decided to try the elevator phone. I picked it up and prepared to punch in the posted emergency number. No dial tone. Not knowing what else to do, I tried clicking my heels together and wishing for home. No, I didn't. But I did try pushing the button for the third floor again while simultaneously jumping up in the air. My idea was that the elevator would start to go up if it believed that it was empty. Surprisingly, my plan didn't work. After a few more minutes, the elevator did begin to move. I was once again released from my prison.

THE MYSTERY CONDIMENT

I like to help my wife by doing certain chores around the house. For example, I make my own breakfast and lunch. On one occasion, I decided to make my favorite sandwich: ham and cheese with pickles and mayonnaise. I gathered all of the ingredients from the refrigerator, placed them on the kitchen table, and prepared my sandwich.

This combination of meat, cheese, and condiments is usually very delicious. This time it seemed to quite bland. When my wife came into the kitchen, I mentioned to her that the mayonnaise had no taste.

"What mayonnaise?" she asked.

I took out the jar, which clearly showed what the contents were. She began to laugh hysterically. After taking a few moments to compose herself, she turned to me and said, "That's not mayonnaise; it's my yeast infection medication!"

Needless to say, I failed to see the humor in it. I asked her, "What person would replace the actual contents of a jar with something else and not indicate what was inside of it?"

My Computer and I Are Not on Speaking Terms

I have a very serious character flaw related to reading and following instructions. *When all else fails, read the instructions* is my philosophy. The following anecdote illustrates the consequences of my failure to read instructions.

When personal computers first appeared in stores, I was not interested in owning one. I resisted the urge to purchase this modern day marvel and saw little benefit that I could derive from its use. But in 1995, I finally succumbed to the idea of possessing one.

I was very excited as I unpackaged the various components and arranged them on my desk. Back when personal computers were becoming popular, there was a tower, a keyboard, speakers, and a mouse. To demonstrate my lack of computer knowledge, I was very surprised to find out that the compact disc tray was NOT a coffee cup holder.

The only thing I knew how to do was turn on the PC. When I finally "booted up", a beautiful bucolic scene appeared on the screen. Within that scene were small figures that I later found out were called *icons*. By clicking on those icons, I was taken to different programs.

I clicked on one and was taken to a program that helped me do all kinds of neat things to the appearance of the screen. For instance, I could change the color, size, and even the shape of what appeared! As I began clicking merrily along in the program, I soon realized that things were getting out of hand. I was in serious trouble. My philosophy of "when all else fails, read the instructions" had come back to haunt me with a vengeance. The trouble was I had no instructions to follow. What to do? Somewhere on the screen was the word *Help*. Yes, that was going to be my way of restoring and reversing the damage I had inflicted on my fresh, out of the box PC.

When I clicked on the help icon, a telephone number appeared. I dialed it, and a male voice answered, "Welcome to the help line. My name is Bob; how may I help you?"

"I just purchased a PC, and I am in a little trouble."

"What is the problem?"

"I started to change the size and shape of my screen saver, and it now looks nothing like it did when I first turned it on."

"What does it look like now?"

"It's concave-shaped on all sides."

"How did it get like that?"

"If I knew that, I wouldn't be calling you."

"Do you see an arrow that moves about when you move the mouse?"

"Yes!"

"Can you click on any icons?"

"There are none."

"Where did they go?"

"You're the expert here."

"I want you to click on the scene on your screen."

"Okay. Uh, oh!"

"What happened?"

"The screen just went blank."

There was a short pause from Bob. "I'm afraid I can't help you. Thank you for calling the help line."

"Thank you! You have been most helpful."

My screen remained blank for almost five weeks. I figured it had somehow gone on a journey inter cyber space. It could have at least sent a postcard...

CHRISTMAS COOKIES

I am not a cook. I can make eggs and bacon. Beyond that, anything I attempt to make turns out to be an experiment. For instance, I thought that baking fish was no big deal. I mean, how hard can it be to open up a package of fish fillets and put them in the stove? As it turned out, it was important to read the directions on the package. That I failed to do. I put the fish into the oven to bake. When I removed the fish from the oven, I was shocked to find that the fillets were still frozen. I picked up the empty package and read the directions- *before baking, separate the fillets.* Who'd have thought?

This brings me to a more recent attempt at baking. It was nearly Christmas Day, so I thought it would be a really good idea to bake some holiday cookies. Wrong! I did have a recipe, and I did follow the directions this time.

How many times had I watched my mother bake? I got all of the ingredients out before me just like my mother did. The recipe called for melted butter, so I put a stick of butter in the microwave for one and a half minutes. The butter exploded and completely drenched the inside of the microwave. Ignoring the foreshadowing of disaster, I continued to make the dough by combining butter, flour, and eggs with a few other ingredients. I spread a layer of flour on the surface of the kitchen counter and another layer on the rolling pin as I had seen my mother do a hundred times before.

As soon as I tried to roll out the dough, it stuck to the rolling pin. Easy solution- just add more eggs. Well, now the dough wasn't firm enough, so I added more flour. This went on for a while- more eggs, then more flour. Since I was mixing the dough by hand on the counter, it wasn't long before it looked like I was wearing gloves! I think I wound up using ten eggs and an indeterminate amount of flour to create a dough ball the size of a melon, but I was finally able to roll the dough out flat. I pulled out my vintage plastic cookie cutters for the next step. I had a heck of a time getting the dough out of the cutters cleanly. (I forgot to dip them in flour first…) When all was said and done, I managed to have a dozen cookies that were almost an inch thick. I placed them on a baking sheet, which I then put in the oven. When they were done, I set them out to cool until morning. When I tried to eat one, I discovered that it was as hard as a brick, so I dunked it in milk.

I told my daughter that I tried to make cookies and hadn't been very successful. She suggested that we try again at Christmas with a different recipe that she had found. When the time came, she got out all of the ingredients, measuring cups and spoons, a rolling pin, and a large mixing bowl and spoon. As she started mixing some of the ingredients together, I queried, "Oh, you're using a bowl? I didn't use a bowl."

She looked at me in surprise and said, "Yeeeeessss… How did you mix your ingredients without a bowl?"

I replied, "I mixed everything with my hands. The recipe didn't say to use a bowl."

She responded, "That's because they assume that you just know to use one!"

I relayed the entire event to her, which she found to be hilarious. We've made cookies at her house every Christmas since then, and I always ask her if we're going to use a bowl.

EVEN SHORTER TRIPS DOWN MEMORY LANE

1. When I was stationed overseas in the Army, I was part owner of an Indian motorcycle. Upon returning to the U.S., I desired to have one of my own. After several years, the opportunity to purchase one presented itself. A friend of mine was selling his bike, so I went to his house and asked to take a test ride. He gave his consent, and I got ready. I kicked the starter, and the bike was ready to go. I put the bike into gear, let out the clutch, gave it some gas, and took off with great speed. In fact, I was unprepared for the abrupt start and panicked. I approached a wire fence, lost my cool, and crashed headfirst into it, causing me to fall with the bike landing on top of me. I was not injured, but the bike had suffered a broken kickstand and mirror. My friend was angry and refused to sell his bike to me. I never entertained the thought of owning a motorcycle again.

2. During most of the 1970s, we lived in a small, single-wide trailer in Edinboro, Pennsylvania. My wife and I shared the one bedroom. Until our two young daughters were in third grade and kindergarten, they shared a tiny room

that was six by five feet. We purchased a small metal bunk bed for them. One day, I had to take the top bunk off for repairs. The bed was held together with bolts that had become rusted over time. There was one nut that I couldn't loosen no matter what I did. The bright idea came to me that I needed heat. I had a butane torch in my tool box, and I figured it would do the trick. I fired up the torch and finally got the nut to turn. I put the torch in my other hand and began to remove the nut. What I didn't notice was that the still-lit torch had set the mattress on fire. Fortunately, I was able to extinguish the flames before setting the whole room ablaze.

3. In the 1970s, there was a severe recession in the States. At one point, my wife was the full-time bread winner, and I played "Mr. Mom" with our two young daughters for a year and a half. Our oldest daughter was in kindergarten, and her class did Show and Tell occasionally. One day, she wanted to take something to show. I made a few suggestions, but she didn't like any of them. Finally, I remembered that I had trapped a mouse the night before. I grabbed a paper bag, dropped the dead mouse in it, and sent her off to school. When she came home that afternoon, I asked her how it went. She replied that her classmates loved it, but the teacher- not so much.

4. As "Mr. Mom", I also cooked some meals for our family. As previously mentioned, I am not a cook, but I did have a surefire way to test spaghetti noodles- toss a strand onto the ceiling. If it falls, you need to cook the noodles longer. If it sticks, then the noodles are ready to serve.

One evening, my wife came home from work, and she was tired and looking forward to dinner. Upon walking into the kitchen, she happened to look up at the ceiling from which several strands of spaghetti were dangling.

She inquired as to why her dinner was suspended from the ceiling.

5. In order to become a member of the fire department, I was required to take drivers' tests for the vehicles that were used. When my turn came, I entered the vehicle with the instructor. It wasn't long before a crowd of onlookers had gathered. As I was backing up, they started yelling at me to watch out. Before I knew what was happening, the instructor also shouted at me to stop. Then I heard a terrible crunching sound as I ran over the instructor's brief case.

6. I am always finding ways to harm myself, but I am a quick learner. For instance, I would admire others when I watched them roller blade, ski, use a bow and arrow, etc. I often overestimate my own ability to do these things. I thought roller blading would be just a simple matter of remaining upright. I put on my newly purchased pair of blades and took off down my street, which had a curved hill at the bottom. I quickly picked up speed as I headed toward the turn. It's amazing how our brains relay to us that we're in serious trouble. As I rounded the corner, I hit some loose stones and found myself two feet in the air and parallel to the ground. As I was about to land, the voice in my head told me to lift my head, which I did just before impact. Once again, I had cheated death (or at least serious injury).

7. I had a husky named Shadow, and we spent a lot of quality time together. We walked almost every day. On one occasion, we were out for a walk, and he suddenly started running. As he was on a leash, I had to keep up with him. Suddenly, there was a telephone pole in our path. He ran left, and I ran right. Just like in the cartoons, I found myself splattered against the pole with my arms on

opposite sides. In addition to the pain from the impact, my watch had somehow been completely destroyed.

8. My oldest daughter and I have enjoyed backpacking, car camping, and hiking in the Rocky Mountains over the years. On one particular occasion, I had flown out to Colorado so that we could do a short backpacking trip in Rocky Mountain National Park. Since we would be above 9,000 feet in elevation, I wanted to be prepared for the low overnight temperatures (which often dipped below freezing), so I had purchased a special sleeping bag ahead of time. It was a German model from World War II. The idea was that sleeping soldiers might need to wake up quickly and be ready to move and fight immediately, so the bags had arm sleeves and bottoms that could be quickly removed. My daughter and I hiked to our first camping spot, set up our two-man tent, and retired for the evening. In the middle of the night, I woke her up as I struggled and thrashed about. She turned on her flashlight, and I explained that I couldn't move my arms and was trapped in my bag. Somehow, the zipper had gotten stuck, and my arms were wrapped around me like a strait jacket! After laughing hysterically, she helped to free me and reminded me that the Germans had lost that war. I eventually fell back to sleep, and the rest of the trip was uneventful. I didn't hold onto that sleeping bag for much longer.

EDDIE'S WORDS OF WISDOM

1. Never put a bark collar around your neck and bark to see if it gives you a shock.
2. When biking down a steep hill, remember not to hit both brakes at the same time.
3. When scuba diving, turn on your air before you submerge. Also, remember to replace your snorkel with your regulator.
4. Never microwave a hamburger in its Styrofoam container.
5. Never use half of a box of laundry powder to wash a load of clothes.
6. Never wash black and white clothes together using hot water in a washing machine.
7. Never use a hot iron on a woolen argyle sweater.
8. When using a coffee maker, be sure to add the coffee.
9. When your car brakes give out, immediately head for a ditch.
10. When running down a dark hallway, don't assume that the bathroom door is open.
11. Always check to see if the furnace is plugged in before you call a repairman.

12. Don't try to adjust the car seat while driving lest ye recline the seat instead.
13. When you have a head cold, never heat Vicks in a sauce pan on high heat.
14. If your wife asks you if she looks heavy, respond instantly. Do not hesitate. Do not lie. Do not look her in the eye. There could have serious consequences.
15. When you disassemble and then reassemble the family stereo console, don't assume that the missing parts will not be found where you hid them.
16. If you see a tire go past you while turning a corner in your car, I suggest you assume that it is yours.
17. When making homemade pickles, don't forget the vinegar.
18. If you fall through the ice while crossing a frozen lake, don't believe that it's a one-time occurrence. (It happened to me again within ten seconds!)
19. If you are fishing without a license, assume that you will get caught.
20. If you've lost your watch in tall grass, it's not a good idea to try to find it by mowing said grass.
21. Don't be offended when you earn a D on a writing assignment and it is returned to you with pizza stains on it.
22. Always check for *One Way* signs before turning onto a road.
23. If you're planning on soaping your neighbors' windows during Halloween, remember this- they could be home even if their lights are off.
24. Always check to make sure that the toilet seat is down before you sit down on it.
25. When you're about to run a hundred mile race in Leadville, Colorado, make sure you leave the Denver airport with your own luggage.

Mud, blood, contusions, bruises!
Now this is why we run and can still smile.

Ed Bray
Rattlesnake 50k - 2009

1990 Laurel High Lands 70 mile run

Finish off 70 mile run: 18hr 56 min

Shoveling snow off the roof in 1993

Photo of the porch after the fire

1996 Punxatawney 50-mile bike race

Printed in the United States
by Baker & Taylor Publisher Services

Printed in the United States
by Baker & Taylor Publisher Services